WHO
IS
JESUS CHRIST?

by
Cooper P. Abrams, III, Ph.D.

Copyright February 2020 by Cooper P. Abrams, III

Who Is Jesus?

Printed in the United States of America. The author of this work has quoted writers of articles and books. This does not mean that the author endorses or recommends the works of others. If the author quotes someone, it does not mean he agrees with all the author's tenets, statements, concepts, or words, whether in the work quoted or any other work.

ISBN 978-1-7344467-3-9

All Scripture taken from the King James Bible.

All rights reserved solely by the author. No part of this work may be reproduced without the expressed consent of the author, except for brief quotes, whether by electronic, photocopying, recording, or information storage and retrieval systems.

Address All Inquiries to:
Cooper P. Abrams, III
Bible Truth Web Site
http://bible-truth.org
435 452-1716
cpabrams3@gmail.com

Published by:
The Old Paths Publications
142 Gold Flume Way
Cleveland, GA 30528
TOP@theoldpathspublications.com
www.theoldpathspublications.com

DEDICATION

This book, with our sincere appreciation, is dedicated to the many individuals and churches who have faithfully prayed and supported the ministry the Lord called us to over the past three decades. God has used their faithfulness and love for souls to be a great encouragement and strength to us in planting churches and winning souls to Christ.

> *"Servants, obey in all things your masters according to the flesh; not with eyeservice, as menpleasers; but in singleness of heart, fearing God: And whatsoever ye do, do it heartily, as to the Lord, and not unto men; Knowing that of the Lord ye shall receive the reward of the inheritance: for ye serve the Lord Christ."* (Colossians 3:22-24)

Cooper and Carolyn Abrams
February 2020

TABLE OF CONTENTS

DEDICATION **3**
TABLE OF CONTENTS 5
Who Is Jesus Christ?... 7
First, He is seen in the Old Testament as the suffering Savior. 15
Second, He is presented as the coming King, the Messiah, and Deliverer....................................... 19
Jesus Christ Is the Word, Our Eternal God, and Savior. 21
All Men Know that God Exists 27
Why Do False Religions And Cults Exist?............ 31
Jesus is God... 35
Jesus Christ is the Creator of the Universe.............. 41
What does the title the "Son of God" mean?....... 45
Jesus is Almighty Jehovah God, the Father, the Eternal God... 49

    Micah 5:2 declares that Jesus the Messiah, is Eternally God... 50

    Jesus is the Father. 51

    The Fact of His Creative Power Proves Conclusively That He Is God, and He is Eternal. 52

Summing up the Bible's Teaching on Jesus Christ..... 59
    This is the Gospel of Jesus Christ................... 59

    What will you do with Jesus right now and where will you spend eternity?............................... 63

    You may pray a simple prayer, honestly with all your heart:.. 69

Who Is Jesus Christ?

"When Jesus came into the coasts of Caesarea Philippi, he asked his disciples, saying, Whom do men say that I the Son of man am? And they said, Some say that thou art John the Baptist: some, Elias; and others, Jeremias, or one of the prophets. He saith unto them, But whom say ye that I am? And Simon Peter answered and said, Thou art the Christ, the Son of the living God. And Jesus answered and said unto him, Blessed art thou, Simon Bar-jona: for flesh and blood hath not revealed it unto thee, but my Father which is in heaven." (Matthew 16:13-17)

With so many different ideas about "Who is Jesus Christ," people need to know the truth. Man's eternal destiny rests on the answer to that question. Jesus Himself warned of believing in false Christs.

"For there shall arise false Christs, and false prophets, and shall shew great signs and wonders; insomuch that, if it were possible, they shall deceive the very elect." (Matthew 24:24)

Even in New Testament times, there were false Christs. The Apostle John wrote,

"Little children, it is the last time: and as ye have heard that antichrist shall come, even now are there many antichrists; whereby we know that it is the last time." (1 John 2:18).

WHO IS JESUS?

The word "antichrist" means "against Christ" or "instead of Christ." The antichrist denies the true Christ and proclaims a substitute. There are also "pseudochristos," meaning a "false Christ," who are imposters. Many claim to follow the Lord Jesus but do not follow or accept what the New Testament teaches about Him. Jesus said,

> *"And many false prophets shall rise, and shall deceive many." (Matthew 24:11)*

Many believe in the teachings and traditions of false teachers and follow them, rather than God's word. Jesus said,

> *"And why call ye me, Lord, Lord, and do not the things which I say?"* (Luke 6:46).

Doing the things Jesus says means to believe and obey His word, the Bible.

Indeed, God has not left us in the dark or even confused as to the answer to the "Who is Jesus Christ?" God has plainly shown His desire and plan to offer man salvation. The Lord desires men to know Him as their Savior because on this vital question rests a person's eternal destiny. Although, men have taught confusing ideas concerning who is Jesus, the Bible is clear. Anyone can know assuredly who Jesus is and how a person can have his or her sins forgiven and become a child of God.

WHO IS JESUS CHRIST?

It is God Himself who explains who the real Christ is: His Son. The New Testament in Acts 4:12 proclaims,

> "Neither is there salvation in any other: for there is none other name under heaven given among men, whereby we must be saved."

The New Testament reveals that Jesus claimed to be the Messiah, our Creator, and Savior of the world. Only He can give man heaven, eternal life, and forgiveness of sins. Without accepting Jesus Christ, a man is eternally condemned.

> "He that believeth on the Son hath everlasting life: and he that believeth not the Son shall not see life; but the wrath of God abideth on him." (John 3:36)

Man is God's creation, and God's word, the Bible, declares that a person must accept the truth of who Jesus truly is and by faith accept Him as their Savior. If a man rejects Him, he will be forever lost. To this vital question, "What then does the Bible say?"

The Bible calls Jesus the "Christ" 58 times in the New Testament. hundred and fifty-eight times, He is called "Jesus Christ." "Christ" is the Greek word for the Hebrew word "Messiah."(John 1:41) (The Greek word is Χριστος or Christos and means anointed, i.e., the Messiah, an epithet of Jesus: — Christ.)

WHO IS JESUS?

In Genesis 3:15, after Adam and Eve sinned, God gave the first Messianic prophecy, which is the first mention of Him sending a Savior to undo the work of Satan. God promised, "And I will put enmity between thee and the woman, and between thy seed and her seed; it shall bruise thy head, and thou shalt bruise his heel."

Note that God referred to Eve's "seed." The reference to "seed" means her offspring. Clearly, God was saying that He would send One (the Messiah - Jesus) who would render a death blow to Satan's head, and undo the results of sin that Satan brought into the world. God also said that Satan would bruise the heel of the seed of the woman, meaning he would oppose and hinder the work of the Messiah. Throughout history, we can see that Satan has been "bruising" Jesus' heel by opposing Him. Although Satan has had a tremendous negative influence in the world, God's plan for man's redemption remains ongoing and unaltered.

How do we know this is correct and that the "seed" is referring to the coming Messiah?

First, what is the meaning of this prophecy? It is clearly about overcoming the work of Satan in tempting Eve and bringing sin into the world. God was giving Adam, Eve,

WHO IS JESUS CHRIST?

and mankind, the assurance that Satan's work would not be successful and go unchecked. The Lord would provide the Savior.

God promised a Savior, the Messiah, meaning "Anointed One." God instructed Samuel to write,

> *"The adversaries of the LORD shall be broken to pieces; out of heaven shall he thunder upon them: the LORD shall judge the ends of the earth; and he shall give strength unto his king, and exalt the horn of his anointed."* (1 Samuel 2:10)

To Abraham, God promised in Genesis 12:3, and 22:17-18, that of his offspring would come One that "in Him, all the nations would be blessed."

> *"Now the LORD had said unto Abram, Get thee out of thy country, and from thy kindred, and from thy father's house, unto a land that I will shew thee: And I will make of thee a great nation, and I will bless thee, and make thy name great; and thou shalt be a blessing: And I will bless them that bless thee, and curse him that curseth thee: and in thee shall all families of the earth be blessed." (Genesis 12:1-3).*

God confirmed His promise saying,

> *"And in thy seed shall all the nations of the earth be blessed; because thou hast obeyed my voice."* (Genesis 22:18).

WHO IS JESUS?

Paul, in Galatians 3:16, confirms that this Promised One, the special offspring of Abraham, identified as "seed" (singular), was the Lord Jesus Christ.

> *"Now to Abraham and his seed were the promises made. He saith not, And to seeds, as of many; but as of one, And to thy seed, which is Christ."* (Galatians 3:16).

Satan, however, as the deceiver offers the world and gullible men, a substitute Messiah made in the image of man.

> *"For the invisible things of him from the creation of the world are clearly seen, being understood by the things that are made, even his eternal power and Godhead; so that they are without excuse: Because that, when they knew God, they glorified him not as God, neither were thankful; but became vain in their imaginations, and their foolish heart was darkened. Professing themselves to be wise, they became fools, And changed the glory of the uncorruptible God into an image made like to corruptible man, and to birds, and fourfooted beasts, and creeping things." (Romans 1:20-23).*

The Apostle John warned about these "antichrists":

> *"Who is a liar but he that denieth that Jesus is the Christ? He is antichrist, that denieth the Father and the Son. Whosoever denieth the Son, the same hath not the Father: (but) he that acknowledgeth the Son hath the Father also."* (1 John 2:22-23)

WHO IS JESUS CHRIST?

In other words, many men have denied the deity of Jesus Christ. False churches and cults have denied that Jesus Christ is God the Father. This article will clearly show that God came to earth, and was incarnated in the man Jesus, and that He is 100% God, and 100% man.

John twice states that Jesus came in the flesh.

> *"Hereby know ye the Spirit of God: Every spirit that confesseth that Jesus Christ is come in the flesh is of God: And every spirit that confesseth not that Jesus Christ is come in the flesh is not of God: and this is that spirit of antichrist, whereof ye have heard that it should come; and even now already is it in the world."* (1 John 4:2-3)

What does the term mean, "Come in the flesh?" John also makes this statement in John 1:14.

> *"And the Word [Logos] was made flesh, and dwelt among us, (and we beheld his glory, the glory as of the only begotten of the Father,) full of grace and truth."* (John 1:14)

Clearly, the Logos (Word) is Jesus Christ. John affirms that Jesus is God, "In the beginning was the Word, and the Word was with God, and the Word was God." (John 1:1)

All men are born in the flesh, so why did John emphasize that Jesus came in the flesh, which means He came as a physical man. The answer is obvious. He states that in stressing the point that Jesus is God, came as a corporeal Being as a human man. That is a marvelous truth, and to deny this clear truth is to deny the deity of Jesus because Jesus being pure and sinless as God could only atone for sin. Man sins against God, and only God can atone and forgive.

Clearly, John said antichrists existed in his day, and they undoubtedly continue to exist in our time also. An "antichrist" is a false Christ, who is an imposter. God has but one "Only Begotten Son," and He is the Lord Jesus Christ, there is no other. The imaginations of man have created many false Christs to be worshiped by gullible men. Men have made their gods like themselves, making them in the likeness of corruptible man, or some creature of the world.

The Old Testament speaks of Christ repeatedly in hundreds of prophecies concerning almost every detail of His Coming. These prophecies concerning His work can be divided into two groups. He is seen as the suffering Savior and as the promised Messiah.

First, He is Seen in the Old Testament as the Suffering Savior.

Psalm 22 is the most quoted Psalm in the Old Testament and clearly speaks of Christ as the rejected and suffering Savior. From verse 6 and following, the passage describes His suffering and reproach. The magnitude of this suffering and the events described are certainly more than David ever experienced, and prophetically predicts the sufferings of Christ.

Psalm 22:6-8 parallels the New Testament account of how that Jesus was scorned in Luke 23:35-36. Matthew 27:38-43 chronicles the Jewish religious leaders' sarcastic sneers, taunting Him, saying,

> "And they that passed by reviled him, wagging their heads, And saying, Thou that destroyest the temple, and buildest it in three days, save thyself. If thou be the Son of God, come down from the cross. Likewise, also the chief priests mocking him, with the scribes and elders, said, He saved others; himself, he cannot save. If he be the King of Israel, let him now come down from the cross, and we will believe him. He trusted in God; let him deliver him now, if he will have him: for he said, I am the Son of God" (Matthew 27:39-43).

Psalm 22:18 predicted what Matthew 27:35 verified in that they parted the Lord's garments.

"They part my garments among them, and cast lots upon my vesture."

John 19:34 records what verse 16 revealed that they pieced Christ's hands and feet.

"For dogs have compassed me: the assembly of the wicked have inclosed me: they pierced my hands and my feet." (Psalms 22:16).

Isaiah 53 is the least quoted passage among the Jews today. This chapter, without question, identifies the promised Messiah, as being the virgin-born Jesus of Nazareth. The passage reveals what the New Testament records emphaticallly that Jesus is the Messiah. The Jews in rejecting Jesus as the Messiah forbid their children from even reading Isaiah 53 because it so graphically and unmistakably refers to the life, work, and death of Jesus. When we read the chapter, one can easily understand why they refuse to read the passage. The passage reveals that the Messiah, with great suffering, would be offered as a lamb led to the slaughter to bear the sins of the world. The Jews, however, were looking for a conquering Messiah, who would give them a worldly kingdom and deliver Israel from the Romans. Jesus did promise them an earthly kingdom, but it will

FIRST, THE SUFFERING SAVIOUR

be inhabited by redeemed Jews who receive their Messiah spiritually in the coming Millennium.

The details of Isaiah 53 reveal that this is speaking of Jesus the Christ. However, Israel did not accept Jesus as their Messiah, who came to save them from their sins and the penalty of death. He offered them a spiritual and a physical kingdom on earth, but they rejected both. Everyone in His kingdom will be there because they believed God's word and sought Him as their spiritual Savior.

WHO IS JESUS?

Second, He is Presented as the Coming King, the Messiah, and Deliverer.

He who would save His people and restore the greatest to Israel.

In Daniel 9:25 Jesus is presented as "the Messiah the Prince."

> *"Seventy weeks are determined upon thy people and upon thy holy city, to finish the transgression, and to make an end of sins, and to make reconciliation for iniquity, and to bring in everlasting righteousness, and to seal up the vision and prophecy, and to anoint the most Holy"* (Daniel 9:24).

Anoint "the most Holy" is a reference to the Messiah coming to establish His promised kingdom.

Isaiah 59:20 says,

> *"And the Redeemer shall come to Zion, and unto them that turn from transgression in Jacob, saith the LORD."*

Throughout history, man has twisted and distorted who Christ is. False teaching, directed by Satan, the master deceiver, Satan has always been represented by false religions, churches, and cults. The Devil has done all he could to discredit and dethrone our God and Savior, the Lord Jesus Christ.

WHO IS JESUS?

The modern cults and false religions of our day were not the first to deny who Jesus Christ truly is. It has been going on since the Fall of Man in the Garden.

Jesus Christ Is the Word, Our Eternal God and Savior.

If something is everlasting, then it has no beginning or end. Does the Bible say that Jesus Christ is our eternal God?

God the Father is our eternal God, and each of the following passages in the New Testament affirms the deity and eternality of Jesus the Christ.

Jesus is God, the Word. (John 1:1, 14)

Jesus Christ is the Word as John 1:1 states,

> *"In the beginning was the Word, and the Word was with God, and the Word was God. The same was in the beginning with God. All things were made by him; and without him was not any thing made that was made."* (John 1:1-3)

John begins by affirming the subject of the Gospel. John is announcing the truth that Jesus Christ is the Logos, our God and Creator. Jesus and His word are the same as He is the Word. He is the Word. John 1:14 affirms the vital truth,

> *"And the Word was made flesh, and dwelt among us, (and we beheld his glory, the glory as of the only begotten of the Father,) full of grace and truth."* (John 1:14)

WHO IS JESUS?

It is vital that when anyone handles, teaches, or preaches God's word the Bible, he does so accurately and without error because handling God's precious Word and Son Jesus Christ. If anyone changes, perverts, distorts, or misuses God's Words, his error is a personal attack on Jesus Himself.

All the modern cults deny the deity of Jesus Christ, which proves them false. They make Him to be only a man. Each of them in different ways states He is only a created being, a good man, a prophet, or that He was a man who became God. Each of these false ideas denies that Jesus is God. However, the Bible, God's word declares He is our God. The Bible, God's word and revelation to us tell us that even as God is eternal, so is Jesus Christ. All the attributes of God the Father are equally attributed to God's Son, Jesus.

Therefore, the Bible explains to us personally who our God and Creator is and tells us who the Lord Jesus Christ is.

Let us then look at the One who one day we will meet and the One who will judge us.

John 17:5 states Jesus is eternal with the Father.

HE IS THE WORD, GOD, & SAVIOUR

"And now, O Father, glorify thou me with thine own self with the glory which I had with thee before the world was."

John 3:16 states,

"For God so loved the world that he gave his only begotten Son, that whosoever believeth in him should not perish, but have everlasting life." You must be eternal to impart everlasting life.

"Simon Peter, a servant and an apostle of Jesus Christ, to them that have obtained like precious faith with us through the righteousness of God and our Saviour Jesus Christ:" (2 Peter 1:1)

1 Timothy 1:17

"Now unto the King eternal, immortal, invisible, the only wise God, be honour and glory for ever and ever. Amen

Titus 2:13

"Looking for that blessed hope, and the glorious appearing of the great God and our Saviour Jesus Christ;"

1 Peter 5:10

"But the God of all grace, who hath called us unto his eternal glory by Christ Jesus, after that ye have suffered a while, make you perfect, stablish, strengthen, settle you."

1 John 5:20

WHO IS JESUS?

> *"And we know that the Son of God is come, and hath given us an understanding, that we may know him that is true, and we are in him that is true, even in his Son Jesus Christ. This is the true God, and eternal life."*

2 Timothy 1:9

> *"Who hath saved us, and called us with a holy calling, not according to our works, but according to his own purpose and grace, which was given us in Christ Jesus before the world began."*

God says that when we savingly believe and put our faith in Him. When a person believes in Jesus Christ and trusts Him as their Savior, He gives that person eternal life and complete forgiveness of sin. To be justified means the penalty for our sins is removed and the believer stands exonerated and declared righteous before God. Justification is a one-time event accomplished by belief in Jesus Christ.

> *"And not as it was by one that sinned, so is the gift: for the judgment was by one to condemnation, but the free gift is of many offenses unto justification. For if by one man's offense death reigned by one; much more they which receive abundance of grace and of the gift of righteousness shall reign in life by one, Jesus Christ.) Therefore, as by the offence of one judgment came upon all men to condemnation; even so by the righteousness of one the free gift came upon all men unto justification of life. For as by one man's*

> *disobedience many were made sinners, so by the obedience of one shall many be made righteous"* (Romans 5:16-19).

The word "justification" is the diakaioma and refers to an acquittal, which renders one innocent, or rightly judged and declared just and righteous by God's divine standard. To justify means, "The act of pronouncing righteous, justification, acquittal." The word "justification" means "a concrete expression of righteousness"; it is a declaration that a person or thing is righteous."

> *"Therefore we conclude that a man is justified by faith without the deeds of the law" (Romans 3:28).*
>
> *"Therefore being justified by faith, we have peace with God through our Lord Jesus Christ:"* (Romans 5:1).
>
> *"Much more then, being now justified by his blood, we shall be saved from wrath through him"* (Romans 5:9).

In John 3:19, Jesus stated why men reject Him.

> *"And this is the condemnation, that light is come into the world, and men loved darkness rather than light, because their deeds were evil. For every one that doeth evil hateth the light, neither cometh to the light, lest his deeds should be reproved. But he that doeth truth cometh to the light, that his deeds may be*

made manifest, that they are wrought in God" (John 3:19-21).

Paul also revealed why men do not accept God's mercy and grace.

"For the wrath of God is revealed from heaven against all ungodliness and unrighteousness of men, who hold the truth in unrighteousness; Because that which may be known of God is manifest in them; for God hath shewed it unto them. For the invisible things of him from the creation of the world are clearly seen, being understood by the things that are made, even his eternal power and Godhead; so that they are without excuse: Because that, when they knew God, they glorified him not as God, neither were thankful; but became vain in their imaginations, and their foolish heart was darkened. Professing themselves to be wise, they became fools, And changed the glory of the uncorruptible God into an image made like to corruptible man, and to birds, and fourfooted beasts, and creeping things" (Romans 1:18-23).

Jesus' deity was plainly demonstrated when He healed the paralyzed man on the Sabbath and forgave His sins.

John 7:14-15

"Now about the midst of the feast Jesus went up into the temple, and taught. And the Jews marveled, saying, How knoweth this man letters, having never learned? Jesus answered them, and said, My doctrine is not mine, but his that sent me."

HE IS THE WORD, GOD, & SAVIOUR

John 7:25-26

"Then said some of them of Jerusalem, Is not this he, whom they seek to kill? But, lo, he speaketh boldly, and they say nothing unto him. Do the rulers know indeed that this is the very Christ?" The word "Christ" means "Messiah."

John 7:40-42

"Many of the people therefore, when they heard this saying, said, Of a truth this is the Prophet. Others said, This is the Christ. But some said, Shall Christ come out of Galilee? Hath not the scripture said, That Christ cometh of the seed of David, and out of the town of Bethlehem, where David was?"

Without question, Jesus established that He was God, incarnate in the flesh.

All Men Know that God Exists

Paul tells us,

"For the wrath of God is revealed from heaven against all ungodliness and unrighteousness of men, who hold the truth in unrighteousness; Because that which may be known of God is manifest in them; for God hath shewed it unto them." (Romans 1:18-19)

Note it says men hold (κατεχω means to suppress) the truth in unrighteousness. Green states it means "to hold down; to detain, retain, Lu. 4.42. Philemon. 13; to hinder, restrain, 2 Th. 2.6, 7; to hold down right, hold in a firm grasp, to have in full and

WHO IS JESUS?

secure possession, 1 Co. 7.30. 2 Co. 6.10; to come into full possession of, seize upon, Mat. 21.38; to keep, retain, 1 Th. 5.21; to occupy, Lu. 14.9; met. . . to hold fast mentally, retain, Lu. 8.15. 1 Co. 11.2; 15.2; to maintain, He. 3.6, 14; 10.23; intrans., a nautical term, to land, touch, Ac. 27.40; pass. . . to be in the grasp of, to be bound by, Ro. 7.6; to be afflicted with, Jno. 5.4."

In verse 20, Paul concludes that men are without excuse because they know or hold the truth in unrighteousness. The truth is plain to see all around them and that God exists and is their Creator, yet they reject this plain truth. Therefore, the existence of God is not the question, but the question is why do men reject Him as their Creator.

Jesus Himself said,

"For the wrath of God is revealed from heaven against all ungodliness and unrighteousness of men, who hold the truth in unrighteousness; Because that which may be known of God is manifest in them; for God hath shewed it unto them." (Romans 1:18-19)

Note it says men hold the truth in unrighteousness. Unrighteousness simply means doing thing wrong, which is sin. In verse 20, Paul concludes that men are without excuse. They know the truth; it is plain to see all around them the evidence of

HE IS THE WORD, GOD, & SAVIOUR

God's creative work, yet they reject God's truth.

"For the invisible things of him from the creation of the world are clearly seen, being understood by the things that are made, even his eternal power and Godhead; so that they are without excuse: Because that, when they knew God, they glorified him not as God, neither were thankful; but became vain in their imaginations, and their foolish heart was darkened. Professing themselves to be wise, they became fools, And changed the glory of the uncorruptible God into an image made like to corruptible man, and to birds, and fourfooted beasts, and creeping things. Wherefore God also gave them up to uncleanness through the lusts of their own hearts, to dishonour their own bodies between themselves: Who changed the truth of God into a lie, and worshipped and served the creature more than the Creator, who is blessed for ever. Amen." (Romans 1:20-25)

WHO IS JESUS?

Why Do False Religions And Cults Exist?

Why do the cults and false religions refuse to accept the deity of Jesus Christ? It is simple. They live in their self-righteousness. They think themselves good enough for heaven or not bad enough for hell. Rarely, will you find a man honest enough to admit he does not deserve heaven. Those who refuse to accept the light are trying by their own good works, church membership, and ordinances to seek to earn a place in Heaven. Yet, God says,

> *"For by grace are ye saved through faith; and that not of yourselves: it is the gift of God: Not of works, lest any man should boast."*
> (Ephesians 2:8-9)

It could not be presented as clear as these verses. You cannot earn heaven which is a free gift of God.

Actually, what they are doing is shunning Christ's love and sacrifice for them and rejecting God's mercy and grace. Jesus shed His sacrificial blood, suffered and died so that man could be forgiven of his sins. They fail to understand that only Jesus Christ can atone for sins, and that He freely offers salvation to all who will believe and trust what He did for them.

WHO IS JESUS?

To reject Jesus Christ and refuse to accept that He is the only Redeemer, exposes man's unworthiness, sin, and depraved sinful nature. Christ being our Creator and Savior, exposes the evil heart of man and shows him to be the sinner he is. Jesus said in John 3:19-20

> *"And this is the condemnation, that light is come into the world, and men loved darkness rather than light, because their deeds were evil. For every one that doeth evil hateth the light, neither cometh to the light, lest his deeds should be reproved."*

Romans 3:10-18, 23 explains the raw truth of the sinfulness of all men.

> *"As it is written, There is none righteous, no, not one:"* (Romans 3:10).

Jesus rebukes those seeking to be worthy of heaven or earn their way to heaven by their church membership, baptism, confirmation, and a host of other works and rituals of man. He warns that man cannot merit or work for his salvation.

God says,

> *"For by grace are ye saved through faith; and that not of yourselves: it is the gift of God: Not of works, lest any man should boast."* (Ephesians 2:8-9).

Obviously, the Lord is saying a man cannot do good works and earn himself a

WHY DO CULTS EXIST?

place in heaven. As a sinner, a man stands in judgment, guilty for his sins. The guilty person cannot free himself or acquit himself. Only a judge or one that has the authority to exonerate can forgive one's crime and set them free. The righteous Judge is Jesus Christ, who has that authority as our God and Creator, and who paid man's sin debt by suffering and dying for sin. Jesus then offers His mercy and grace to all who will believe and by faith accept His atonement and full payment for sins.

John states,

"And he (Jesus) is the propitiation (full payment) for our sins: and not for ours only, but also for the sins of the whole world." (1 John 2:2).

As Romans 3:10 affirms,

"There is none righteous, no not one."

In the light of Jesus Christ's deity is the revealed truth that man can offer nothing for his salvation and that man's works and righteousness are as "filthy rags." Isaiah wrote,

"But we are all as an unclean thing, and all our righteousnesses are as filthy rags; and we all do fade as a leaf; and our iniquities, like the wind, have taken us away." (Isaiah 64:6).

Man is not the savior! Man can do nothing to save himself and it is foolish if he

WHO IS JESUS?

persists in trying to offer the "filthy rags" of good deeds and religious rituals for his salvation. How tragic that a man would offer his own unrighteousness, instead of the pure shed blood of our Holy and All Righteous God, the Lord Jesus Christ. Oh, the tragedy of such foolishness that denies the truth and believes Satan's lies that condemn a man to hell.

Jesus is God.

John proclaimed Jesus is God in John 1:1-3, 14 In John 8:58, Jesus ended His discourse to these false religious leaders and proclaimed, *"Verily, verily I say unto you, Before Abraham was, I AM."*

The exclamation "I am" is the Hebrew word 'Yehyeh (pronounced eh-yeh); the name Yahweh is actually the third person form of the verb and would translate "He is." Worshipers declare, "He is!" However, God explains that it means "I am," I am the self-existent One. In light of so many denying that Jesus is God, He simply declares, I AM!

Without question, Jesus claimed to be Jehovah God. The Jews knew the name "I Am" well because when Moses asked God whom he should tell the children of Israel had sent him to lead them out of Egypt this is what the Lord replied. Exodus 3:14 records,

"And God said unto Moses, I AM THAT I AM:

and he said,

Thus shalt thou say unto the children of Israel, I AM hath sent me unto you."

They knew this was who Moses said had spoken to him and led them out of Egypt. Jesus said he was God the Father,

WHO IS JESUS?

> *"Jesus said unto them, Verily, verily, I say unto you, Before Abraham was, I am."* (John 8:58)

The Jews knew that only God can forgive sin. By forgiving sin Jesus proclaimed He was God and the Jews who were rejecting Jesus as the Messiah said He had blasphemed against God.

Understanding Jesus' statement as blasphemy (claiming to be God), they rioted and took up stones to kill Jesus; however, Jesus alluded them and passed through their midst unharmed.

Jesus was saying He was Jehovah God, the "Self-Existent One, and Eternal One." He identified Himself as the One who sent Moses to the Children of Israel when they were in captivity in Egypt. Again in John 10:24, when the Jews asked Jesus to tell them plainly if He was the Messiah, He responded: *"I and my Father are one."* (John 10:30) Jesus had explained that

> *"My sheep hear my voice, and I know them, and they follow me: And I give unto them eternal life; and they shall never perish, neither shall any man pluck them out of my hand."* (John 10:27-28)

Only God can give eternal life, and understanding Jesus' proclamation of His deity; they took up stones to kill Him. Jesus asked them why they sought to stone Him.

HE IS GOD

"The Jews answered him, saying, For a good work we stone thee not; but for blasphemy; and because that thou, being a man, makest thyself God." (John 10:33).

1. The Jews had seen over twenty-five different supernatural miracles that Jesus had done, yet they still would not accept Him. Jesus in John 9:1-12, on the Sabbath, healed the man born blind thus demonstrating that He was God. It was God who gave Israel the Sabbath. Exodus 16:29 states,

"See, for that the LORD hath given you the sabbath, therefore he giveth you on the sixth day the bread of two days; abide ye every man in his place, let no man go out of his place on the seventh day."

The word LORD is the word "Jehovah" establishing that Jehovah God gave the Sabbath. Jesus being God is Jehovah God of the Sabbath and the Master of the Sabbath. He was in control of the Sabbath being its Creator and had the right to do what pleased Him. Matthew 12:8 declares

"For the Son of man is Lord even of the sabbath day."

2. In John 9:13 the Jews brought the once blind man before the Pharisees and questioned him. Note verse 16.

"Therefore said some of the Pharisees, This man is not of God, because he keepeth not the sabbath day. Others said, How can a man that

WHO IS JESUS?

is a sinner do such miracles? And there was a division among them." (John 9:16).

Jesus had just healed a blind man. They plainly saw Jesus demonstrate His power as God. Some proposed the question, "How can a man that is a sinner do such miracles?" They knew and recognized that Jesus was not a sinner. This is the first time in the history of the world that this happened. Further, this fulfilled the Messianic prophecy of Isaiah 35:5-6:

> *"Then the eyes of the blind shall be opened, and the ears of the deaf shall be unstopped. Then shall the lame man leap as an hart, and the tongue of the dumb sing: for in the wilderness shall waters break out, and streams in the desert."*

3. They knew this was an unprecedented miracle. Seeking some way out and refusing to accept what they had without question seen, they asked the healed man's parents was this truly their son. Why was all the fuss? They knew very well that only God could do such a miracle. His parents identified him yet would not state how he was healed. They said he is a grown man, ask him.

4. Again, they questioned the blind man in verses 24-29. The healed man rebuked the Pharisees, saying,

HE IS GOD

"He answered them, I have told you already, and ye did not hear: wherefore would ye hear it again? will ye also be his disciples? Then they reviled him, and said, Thou art his disciple; but we are Moses' disciples. We know that God spake unto Moses: as for this fellow, we know not from whence he is." (John 9:27-29).

5. Listen to the testimony of the man in verses 30-33.

"The man answered and said unto them, Why herein is a marvelous thing, that ye know not from whence he is, and yet he hath opened mine eyes. Now we know that God heareth not sinners: but if any man be a worshipper of God, and doeth his will, him he heareth. Since the world began was it not heard that any man opened the eyes of one that was born blind. If this man were not of God, he could do nothing" (John 9:30-33).

6. When Jesus heard of how the Pharisees had treated the man, He went to see Him. Jesus asks him. (V35). *"Do you believe on the Son of God?"* The man then asks Jesus, *"Who is he, Lord, that I might believe him."*

Then Jesus emphatically affirmed who He was by stating, *"Thou hast both seen him, and it is he that talked with thee"* (V37). Jesus Himself proclaimed that He was God. To deny Jesus is God is calling Him a liar.

Then at that moment, a lost sinner was saved, and for all eternity, because he believed in Jesus Christ and worshiped Him. "And he said,

WHO IS JESUS?

Lord, I believe. And he worshipped him." (John 9:38).

Jesus accepted his worship because He is God.

Jesus Christ is the Creator of the Universe.

It is dumbfounding that the deity of Jesus is questioned when the Bible, written under inspiration of God,

> *"In the beginning was the Word, and the Word was with God, and the Word was God. The same was in the beginning with God. All things were made by him; and without him was not anything made that was made. In him was life; and the life was the light of men." (John 1:1)*

(Concerning the inspiration of the scriptures see 2 Tim. 3:16-17, 2 Peter 1:21)

John 1:14 clears up any misunderstanding concerning whom the Word is.

> *"And the Word was made flesh, and dwelt among us, (and we beheld his glory, the glory as of the only begotten of the Father) full of grace and truth."*

John 1:1 declares the "Word" (Logos) was God. Verse 14 explains that the Logos was made flesh and *"dwelt among us"* that is an unmistakable reference to Jesus Christ. This is the meaning of the title "only begotten." God came to earth incarnate in flesh.

WHO IS JESUS?

What does the title "only begotten" mean?"

The title "only begotten" is found six times in scripture and each time of Jesus Christ. (See John 1:14, 18; 3:16, 18; Heb. 11:17; 1 John 4:9.)

The phrase "only begotten" is monogenes "mon-og-en-ace.'" "mono" means "only one" and "gen-ace" meaning, "to beget." "Beget" is the word the Greek dictionaries and lexicon use, but a better definition is that Jesus "emanated" from the Father, that means "to flow out, issue, or proceed, as from a source or origin; come forth; originate." The Greek text reads "the Son the only Begotten" (ton huion ton monogenê)." This statement is exclusively used of the Lord Jesus and states absolutely that God the Father has no other begotten Son. In other words, Jesus Christ is unique in being God incarnate as man. The phrase is not saying Jesus is the offspring of God the Father, but rather is the same with the Father. Neither, can the phrase mean Jesus was God's created Son.

To reiterate this truth, the phrase *"only begotten of the Father"* affirms the deity and uniqueness of Jesus Christ a being God incarnate in Man. They are one and the same. Further, the phrase precludes that no man is

HE IS THE CREATOR

the "only begotten of God the Father." The late Henry Morris explained,

> "As monotheism connotes only one God and monosyllable means a word of only one syllable, so monogenes means only one genesis or only one generated-- or, more simply, only begotten... It does not mean "one," or even "one and only" It is worth noting that, although Christ is called the Son, or Son of God, frequently in the New Testament, He is never (in the Greek original) called the "only" son of God." It means as the Son of God and it cannot be understood that Jesus had a beginning. He is Alpha and Omega, meaning eternal. He was not created, but is the incarnation of God the Father. Jesus Christ is God the Father incarnated. Incarnated states that God the Father was in human form. (See John 14:7-9)"

John 1:1-3 tells us that Jesus was conceived by the Holy Spirit and born of a virgin. This explains how God became a man. Our God and Creator came to earth and dwelled among men. Jesus Christ is as Colossians 1:15-17 explains,

"Who is the image of the invisible God, the firstborn of every creature: For by him were all things created, that are in heaven, and that are in earth, visible and invisible, whether they be thrones, or dominions, or principalities, or powers: all things were created by him, and for

WHO IS JESUS?

him: And he is before all things, and by him all things consist" (Colossians 1:15-17).

Certainly, it is clear what the phrase *"Who is the image of the invisible God"* means. An image can be seen, however, God is invisible, thus the verse says that Jesus is visible God. Jesus confirms this truth, saying, *"I and my Father are one."* (John 10:30).

What does the Title the "Son of God" Mean?

John says Jesus is God, and all things were made by Him. This is why Jesus is called the "Son of God" and "only begotten Son." God was incarnated as a man through the Holy Spirit, thus He was fully a man being born unto Mary. Jesus was wholly God and man.

The term "son of God" occurs more than 40 times in the Bible, all of them in the New Testament. The phrase is found in the KJV in Daniel 3:25, but the Hebrew word for God is actually in the plural, so it means, "son of the gods." So, what do we find when we examine the phrase in the New Testament?

1. Jesus Christ is the Son of God, (Matt. 26:63; Mark 1:1; John 20:31; Heb. 4:14).
2. Unclean spirits would fall down before Jesus and say, "You are the Son of God," (Mark 3:11).
3. ". . . The holy offspring shall be called the Son of God," (Luke 1:35).
4. Adam is said to be the son of God (Luke 3:38).
5. Those who hear the voice of the Son of God shall live (John 5:25).
6. Paul had faith in the Son of God (Gal. 2:20).

WHO IS JESUS?

> 7. Son of God has no beginning or end (Heb. 7:3).
> 8. The Son of God appeared to destroy the works of the devil (1 John 3:8).
> 9. Believing in the Son of God so that you may have eternal life (1 John 5:13)."

The Bible proclaims that Jesus is God and that He and the Father are one and the same as He stated in John 10:30. Isaiah affirmed this truth in Isaiah 7:14 and 9:6, predicting the coming Messiah.

> *"Therefore the Lord himself shall give you a sign; Behold, a virgin shall conceive, and bear a son, and shall call his name Immanuel."* (Isaiah 7:14)

The name "Immanuel'" means "God with us" as Matthew 1:23 affirms. Isaiah 9:6 states

> *"For unto us a child is born, unto us a son is given: and the government shall be upon his shoulder: and his name shall be called Wonderful, Counseller, The mighty God, The everlasting Father, The Prince of Peace."* (Isaiah 9:6).

The title "Son of God" cannot be physical because overwhelmingly, Jesus is revealed to be our eternal Creator who is God. Jesus is the eternal God and Creator and was not created. Not being created, he could not be the physical Son of the Father who is Spirit; thus, the title means something

WHAT DOES "SON OF GOD" MEAN

else. As stated earlier, Jesus is God the Father incarnated physically in God the Son. It simply conveys the truth that Jesus is God, co-equal with God the Father, being His Son.

Appearing to Mary, the angel proclaimed,

> *"And the angel answered and said unto her, The Holy Ghost shall come upon thee, and the power of the Highest shall overshadow thee: therefore also that holy thing which shall be born of thee shall be called the Son of God."* (Luke 1:35)

The angel calls Jesus the "Son of God," which establishes His relationship to God the Father. Isaiah states that Jesus' name is Immanuel. (Isa. 7:14) To Joseph the angel announced this name would be Emmanuel, meaning "God with us."

> *"Behold, a virgin shall be with child, and shall bring forth a son, and they shall call his name Emmanuel, which being interpreted is, God with us."* (Matthew 1:23)

The statements can only be understood as stating the Jesus was the incarnation of God the Father.

When Jesus was illegally tried before the Jewish high court He was asked was He the Christ? Jesus answers saying,

> *"Art thou the Christ? tell us. And he said unto them, If I tell you, ye will not believe: And if I*

WHO IS JESUS?

also ask you, ye will not answer me, nor let me go. Hereafter shall the Son of man sit on the right hand of the power of God. Then said they all, Art thou then the Son of God? And he said unto them, Ye say that I am. And they said, What need we any further witness? for we ourselves have heard of his own mouth." (Luke 22:67-71)

Note that Jesus stated He would later be sitting at the right hand of the power of God. His statement *"Ye say that I am"* confirmed to the Jews that Jesus' answer was in the affirmative. He declared He was the Son of God and the Jews understood He was professing His deity.

Jesus is Almighty Jehovah God, the Father, the Eternal God.

1. Isaiah could not state this fact any clearer when he wrote,

"For unto us a child is born, unto us a son is given: and the government shall be upon his shoulder: and his name shall be called Wonderful, Counseller, The mighty God, The everlasting Father, The Prince of Peace. Of the increase of his government and peace there shall be no end, upon the throne of David, and upon his kingdom, to order it, and to establish it with judgment and with justice from henceforth even for ever. The zeal of the LORD of hosts will perform this" (Isaiah 9:6-7).

The word LORD is Jehovah.

Note,

"No man hath seen God at any time; the only begotten Son, which is in the bosom of the Father, he hath declared him." (John 1:18).

2. Revelation 19:11-13 also emphatically identifies who is the Word.

"And I saw heaven opened, and behold a white horse; and he that sat upon him was called Faithful and True, and in righteousness he doth judge and make war. His eyes were as a flame of fire, and on his head were many crowns; and he had a name written, that no man knew, but he himself. And he was clothed with a vesture

WHO IS JESUS?

dipped in blood: and his name is called The Word of God." (Revelation 19:11-13).

3. There is no doubt or any room in the Bible's statements other than that Jesus Christ is the eternal God, He is the Word, and He is everlasting.

4. Jesus in the Book of Revelation, proclaims that He is eternal.

"I am Alpha and Omega, the beginning and the ending, saith the Lord, which is, and which was, and which is to come, the Almighty." (Rev. 1:8).

"I am Alpha and Omega, the beginning and the end, the first and the last." (Revelation 22:13) (Also, see Rev. 1:11, 21:6)

Micah 5:2 declares that Jesus the Messiah, is eternally God.

"But thou, Bethlehem E-ph-rat-ah, though thou be little among the thousands of Judah, yet out of thee shall he come forth unto me that is to be ruler in Israel; whose goings forth have been from of old, from everlasting." (Micah 5:2)

This is a prophecy of the coming of the Messiah. As already shown the Messiah is Jesus Christ and Jesus at His human birth was declared to be "God with us." (Matt. 1:23)

JESUS IS ALMIGHTY JEHOVAH

Jesus is the Father.

Jesus in John 14 told his disciples that He would be leaving them and returning to heaven.

> *"Jesus saith unto him, I am the way, the truth, and the life: no man cometh unto the Father, but by me. If ye had known me, ye should have known my Father also: and from henceforth ye know him, and have seen him. Philip saith unto him, Lord, shew us the Father, and it sufficeth us. Jesus saith unto him, Have I been so long time with you, and yet hast thou not known me, Philip? he that hath seen me hath seen the Father; and how sayest thou then, Shew us the Father? Believest thou not that I am in the Father, and the Father in me? the words that I speak unto you I speak not of myself: but the Father that dwelleth in me, he doeth the works. Believe me that I am in the Father, and the Father in me: or else believe me for the very works' sake"* (John 14:6-11).

Note Jesus' answer to Philip when he asked Him to show them the Father: *"Philip saith unto him, Lord, shew us the Father, and it sufficeth us."* Jesus was confirming again what He had told His disciple in John 10:38

> *"But if I do, though ye believe not me, believe the works: that ye may know, and believe, that the Father is in me, and I in him."* (John 10:38).

> *"Jesus saith unto him, Have I been so long time with you, and yet hast thou not known me, Philip? he that hath seen me hath seen the*

WHO IS JESUS?

Father; and how sayest thou then, Shew us the Father?" (John 14:9).

Without question, Jesus said that He was the Father. They, seeing Him physically, were seeing God the Father incarnate in man.

The Fact of His Creative Power Proves Conclusively That He Is God, and He is Eternal.

The Gospel of John proclaims our Creator as being Jesus Christ.

"All things were made by him; And without him was not anything made that was made." (John 1:3).

The verb "was made" means, "came into being." It is significant because it literally means, "it came into being out of nothing." The phrase "came out of nothing" is the word "exhilo." This single verse refutes every form of evolution. It establishes the origin of the Universe and all life as coming from God in His creative act. God the Father is revealed in Genesis 1:1 as the Creator and coupled with this verse proves Jesus, and the Father are One.

Hebrews 1:3, 10, proclaims Christ as the Creator.

"Who being the brightness of his glory, and the express image of his person, and upholding all things by the word of his power, when he had by himself purged our sins, sat down on the

JESUS IS ALMIGHTY JEHOVAH

right hand of the Majesty on high; And, Thou, Lord, in the beginning hast laid the foundation of the earth; and the heavens are the works of thine hands."

"Who is the image of the invisible God, the firstborn of every creature: For by him were all things created, that are in heaven, and that are in earth, visible and invisible, whether they be thrones, or dominions, or principalities, or powers: all things were created by him, and for him: And he is before all things, and by him all things consist." (Colossians 1:15-17).

Acts 17:28 explains that all mankind is Jesus' creation.

"For in him we live, and move, and have our being; as certain also of your own poets have said, For we are also his offspring." (Acts 17:28).

Psalm 96:4-5 acknowledges that Jehovah is the only God. The word "LORD" is Jehovah, referring to God in the Person of the Father.

"For the LORD is great, and greatly to be praised: he is to be feared above all gods. For all the gods of the nations are idols: but the LORD made the heavens. Honour and majesty are before him: strength and beauty are in his sanctuary." (Psalms 96:4-6).

Psalm 115:15 confirmed that. Jehovah God the Father made the heavens.

WHO IS JESUS?

> *"Ye are blessed of the LORD which made heaven and earth. The heaven, even the heavens, are the LORD'S: but the earth hath he given to the children of men."* (Psalms 115:15-16).

Also, Isaiah 42:5 reaffirms that Jehovah made the heavens, earth, and gave life to men.

> *"Thus saith God the LORD, he that created the heavens, and stretched them out; he that spread forth the earth, and that which cometh out of it; he that giveth breath unto the people upon it, and spirit to them that walk therein:"* (Isaiah 42:5).

When we note the many verses that assert that Jesus Christ created all things and that Jehovah, God the Father is also revealed as the Creator the conclusion is clear and definite. God the Father and Jesus Christ are One and the Creator and only God could atone for sin and offer His free gift of forgiveness and eternal life.

The Bible stresses that one day every man will meet Jesus face to face. This is why this message is so important, because every man, woman, boy or girl in the world will someday meet Him face to face. Both those who love and accept Him as their Savior and those who reject Him will one day stand before Him.

JESUS IS ALMIGHTY JEHOVAH

"For it is written, As I live, saith the Lord, every knee shall bow to me, and every tongue shall confess to God." (Romans 14:11)

Philippians 2:10

"That at the name of Jesus every knee should bow, of things in heaven, and things in earth, and things under the earth; And that every tongue should confess that Jesus Christ is Lord, to the glory of God the Father."

Hebrews 12:23-29 declares that Jesus is the Judge of "all."

"To the general assembly and church of the firstborn, which are written in heaven, and to God the Judge of all, and to the spirits of just men made perfect, And to Jesus the mediator of the new covenant, and to the blood of sprinkling, that speaketh better things than that of Abel. See that ye refuse not him that speaketh. For if they escaped not who refused him that spake on earth, much more shall not we escape, if we turn away from him that speaketh from heaven: Whose voice, then shook the earth: but now he hath promised, saying, Yet once more I shake not the earth only, but also heaven. And this word, Yet once more, signifieth the removing of those things that are shaken, as of things that are made, that those things which cannot be shaken may remain. Wherefore we receiving a kingdom which cannot be moved, let us have grace, whereby we may serve God acceptably with reverence and godly fear: For our God is a consuming fire." (Hebrews 12:23-29).

WHO IS JESUS?

Romans 14:11,

"For it is written, As I live, saith the Lord, every knee shall bow to me, and every tongue shall confess to God."

Philippians 2:10

"That at the name of Jesus every knee should bow, of things in heaven, and things in earth, and things under the earth;"

When you meet Him will it be as His obedient child? Will you stand before Him, forgiven of your sins and unashamed having put your faith and trust in Him as your personal Savior? (See Rom. 8:16-17, 9:7)

On the other hand, if you refuse to believe and accept Him, will you stand before Him condemned because you have rejected His grace and sacrifice for you. James 4:4 says that those refuse to believe and that love the world is actually His enemy. (Read James 4:4-10)

John 3:36 says,

"He that believeth on the Son hath everlasting life: and he that believeth not the Son shall not see life; but the wrath of God abideth on him."

In this verse, there are two truths. It pronounces that those who believe have everlasting life. Further, it declares that those who do not believe do not have life and the wrath of God abideth on them. In other words, they will be eternally separated from God in hell.

> *"And to you who are troubled rest with us, when the Lord Jesus shall be revealed from heaven with his mighty angels, In flaming fire taking vengeance on them that know not God, and that obey not the gospel of our Lord Jesus Christ: Who shall be punished with everlasting destruction from the presence of the Lord, and from the glory of his power,"* (2 Thessalonians 1:7-9).

It is our choice to believe God's word and to put our faith in His promise of forgiveness of sins and eternal life. If one does nothing, God tells us we will stand before Him in the judgment being condemned.

However, the Good News (Gospel) is: if we believe and simply trust Him, we will have life eternal. God promises salvation to all who believe what He has recorded for us in the Bible. If in belief, we accept Him as our Savior, we will stand before Him as a friend, as our loving Savior with whom we will spend eternity. We are absolutely assured of our redemption in Christ because of His sacrifice for us. God promises that heaven will be our home, and we will be joint-heirs with Jesus Christ. (See Rom. 8:17)

WHO IS JESUS?

Jesus promised,

"That whosoever believeth in him should not perish, but have eternal life. For God so loved the world, that he gave his only begotten Son, that whosoever believeth in him should not perish, but have everlasting life. For God sent not his Son into the world to condemn the world; but that the world through him might be saved. He that believeth on him is not condemned: but he that believeth not is condemned already, because he hath not believed in the name of the only begotten Son of God. And this is the condemnation, that light is come into the world, and men loved darkness rather than light, because their deeds were evil. For every one that doeth evil hateth the light, neither cometh to the light, lest his deeds should be reproved. But he that doeth truth cometh to the light, that his deeds may be made manifest, that they are wrought in God." (John 3:15-21).

The Good News is that no one needs to stand before God in condemnation. Our loving God and Savior offers His mercy and grace to all who will believe and by faith accept Him as their Savior. He forgives all of a person's sins completely and gives that believer eternal life.

Summing up the Bible's Teaching on Jesus Christ

God the Father is the Creator of the Universe and of us all as Genesis 1-2 records. Here we have seen that the Bible states that Jesus is the Christ, the Savior, our God and Creator, God the Son, wholly man and wholly God. Seeing that God and Jesus Christ are revealed to be the Creator, then plainly, the Word of God is proclaiming that Jesus and God the Father are One. The importance of this truth is that if a person believes and puts his faith in Jesus Christ, he will be forgiven of his sins and receive eternal life. This is why God, the Lord Jesus, came to earth. Paul stated it clearly, *"This is a faithful saying, and worthy of all acceptation, that Christ Jesus came into the world to save sinners; of whom I am chief."* (1 Timothy 1:15). Luke also confirms the reason God came to earth *"For the Son of man is come to seek and to save that which was lost."* (Luke 19:10). That means Jesus came to provide salvation for you and me.

This is the Gospel of Jesus Christ.

Paul stressed the Gospel, which he preached and taught.

> *"Moreover, brethren, I declare unto you the gospel which I preached unto you, which also ye have received, and wherein ye stand; By*

WHO IS JESUS?

> *which also ye are saved, if ye keep in memory what I preached unto you, unless ye have believed in vain. For I delivered unto you first of all that which I also received, how that Christ died for our sins according to the scriptures; And that he was buried, and that he rose again the third day according to the scriptures:*" (1 Corinthians 15:1-4)

Jesus came to earth, suffered, and died to pay the penalty for our sins. He proved He was God when He rose from the grave, victorious over sin and death. (See 1 Cor. 15:55-57). It is a vital truth that only God is perfect and without sin and could only offer Himself for the atonement of sins. Jesus being God, the second member of the Trinity, is sinless because He is God. Paul, Peter, and John proclaimed the sinlessness of Jesus:

> *"For he hath made him to be sin for us, who knew no sin; that we might be made the righteousness of God in him."* (2 Corinthians 5:21)

> *"Who did no sin, neither was guile found in his mouth:"* (1 Peter 2:22)

> *"And ye know that he was manifested to take away our sins; and in him is no sin."* (1 John 3:5)

Jesus is seeking to save us from our sins and give us His free gift of eternal life in heaven with Him. His purpose is that we would accept His sacrifice for us.

SUMMING UP THE TEACHING

"For the Son of man is come to seek and to save that which was lost." (Luke 19:10).

We should not be mistaken. God is strongly speaking to each of us today by His word; even now, He is seeking the lost. He asked the once blind man, *"Dost thou believe in the Son of God?"* (John 9:35). This is His present question to each of us.

This is the most important question a man or woman will ever answer. The man who saw Jesus Christ was healed, he believed, and worshiped the Lord. His body was not only healed, but also His soul, in that his sins were forgiven. Only God is worshiped and never any man. Jesus accepted the man's worship because He was God.

If you have not accepted Jesus Christ as your Savior, will you now, today, believe and accept the Lord Jesus Christ? Will you believe in God, our Lord and Savior, accept His promises, and be forgiven of your sins and receive eternal life? The answer is yours to make!

You will see Him one day face to face as God tells us,

"For it is written, As I live, saith the Lord, every knee shall bow to me, and every tongue shall confess to God." (Romans 14:11).

WHO IS JESUS?

He says to us,

"The Lord is not slack concerning his promise, as some men count slackness; but is longsuffering to us-ward, not willing that any should perish, but that all should come to repentance." (2 Peter 3:9).

Paul tells believers,

"For we know that if our earthly house of this tabernacle were dissolved, we have a building of God, a house not made with hands, eternal in the heavens...Therefore we are always confident, knowing that, whilst we are at home in the body, we are absent from the Lord:" (2 Corinthians 5:1, 6)

For those who believe it will be a wonderful day that will last throughout eternity.

It means Christians will come before Him as a friend, and it will be a time of reward and joy as the Savior says, *"Well done my beloved servant...."* On the other hand, for Christians who were not faithful to the Lord in their lives, it will be a time of shame as they realized what they lost.

"If any man's work abide which he hath built thereupon, he shall receive a reward. If any man's work shall be burned, he shall suffer loss: but he himself shall be saved; yet so as by fire." (1 Corinthians 3:14-15).

What it means for the believer is that it will be a time of happiness knowing he

SUMMING UP THE TEACHING

received Christ's forgiveness; that all his sins are forgiven.

Would you now agree with God's word, that this is the most important truth on earth today? The most important question you and I must ask .. . .

What will you do with Jesus right now and where will you spend eternity?

If you should die today, do you know where you would spend eternity? The person who puts his faith and trust in Jesus as Savior and God alone for the forgiveness of his sins knows he will be in heaven. He knows that when he dies, he will instantly wake up in heaven. This is based on the promise of God's character in that He cannot lie. No one likes to think about dying, but death comes to everyone. Death for all is a stark reality. God tells us in His Word,

> "...It is appointed unto men once to die, but after this the judgment:" (Hebrews 9:27).

Yet, God is merciful and gracious and, at this moment, is giving us the opportunity to prepare to meet God in salvation.

According to God's Word, everyone will spend eternity in one of two places-- either in heaven or in hell.

WHO IS JESUS?

> *"And these shall go away into everlasting punishment* (hell): *but the righteous into life eternal* (heaven)." (Matthew 25:46).

Every person born inherited a sinful nature.

> *"Wherefore, as by one man (Adam) sin entered into the world, and death by sin; and so death passed upon all men, for that all have sinned:"* (Romans 5:12). *"... and were by nature the children of wrath, even as others."* (Ephesians 2:3b).

> *"Behold, I was shapen in iniquity; and in sin did my mother conceive me."* (Psalm 51:5). *"The heart is deceitful above all things, and desperately wicked: who can know it?"* (Jeremiah 17:9).

This sinful nature produces all sorts of sin in our lives.

> *"For from within, out of the heart of men, proceed evil thoughts, adulteries, fornications, murders, thefts, covetousness; wickedness, deceit, lasciviousness, an evil eye, blasphemy, pride, foolishness: all these evil things come from within, and defile the man."* (Mark 7:21-23).

The New Testament records the question of a Roman jailer who guarded the imprisoned Paul. When he recognized himself as a sinner, he asked, *"Sirs, what must I do to be saved?"* The answer is simple:

SUMMING UP THE TEACHING

First, a person must confess that they are a sinner and admit it not only to themselves but also to God. To be saved, a person must acknowledge they have sinned against God and seek His forgiveness. Sin separates us from God's grace, mercy, and salvation. God's Word declares this truth.

> "That if thou shalt confess with thy mouth the Lord Jesus, and shalt believe in thine heart that God hath raised him from the dead, thou shalt be saved." (Romans 10:9)

Because we all are sinners, we are destined for hell for all eternity.

> "For the wages of sin is death..." (Romans 6:23). "... and sin, when it is finished, bringeth forth death." (James 1: 15).

There is nothing you can do to save yourself except to believe and in repentance ask God to save you. We cannot be good enough. "... there is none that doeth good, no, not one." (Romans 3:12). No one can be saved by keeping the law or doing good works. Joining a church, doing religious rituals, and being baptized will not save you. God says,

> "For by grace are ye saved through faith; and that not of yourselves: it is the gift of God: Not of works, lest any man should boast." (Ephesians 2:8-9).

Grace means unmerited favor. Paul explained,

WHO IS JESUS?

> *"Not by works of righteousness which we have done, but according to his mercy he saved us, by the washing of regeneration, and renewing of the Holy Ghost;"* (Titus 3:5).

To the Galatians who were seeking to earn their salvation by their works, Paul wrote *"... By the works of the law shall no flesh be justified."* (Galatians 2: 16). All this means that we are helpless and cannot save ourselves, but our gracious Savior Jesus Christ can and will if we believe.

> *"That if thou shalt confess with thy mouth the Lord Jesus, and shalt believe in thine heart that God hath raised him from the dead, thou shalt be saved. For with the heart man believeth unto righteousness; and with the mouth confession is made unto salvation."* (Romans 10:9-10).

Jesus is the only one who could pay our sin debt being our sinless and holy God. That is what he did on the cross. What foolishness and tragedy it is for anyone to think he could do what Jesus has already done. To think a person can offer his works for his salvation is to mock and belittle who Jesus is, His grace, and suffering and death and God's plan of salvation.

However, there is the Good News of the Gospel. In spite of our sin, .and the false ideas of sinful men, God loves us and has done everything necessary for our salvation.

SUMMING UP THE TEACHING

"For when we were yet without strength (helpless), in due time Christ died for the ungodly...But God commendeth his love toward us, in that, while we were yet sinners, Christ died for us." (Romans 5:6, 8).

God tells us in His word,

"For Christ also hath once suffered for sins, the just for the unjust, that he might bring us to God, being put to death in the flesh, but quickened by the Spirit:" (1 Peter 3: 18).

Just believing intellectually that you are a sinner, that God loves you, and that Christ died for you is not enough. James explains,

"Thou believest that there is one God; thou doest well: the devils also believe, and tremble." (James 2:19).

You must believe and commit this truth to yourself personally by repenting and receiving the Lord Jesus Christ as your own Saviour. Repentance is a change of mind brought to your heart by the Holy Spirit, through the Word of God. It causes a person to see the truth of their sinful state and then in faith turn from their sins, from dead religions, and works to trust Christ alone.

God proclaims in His word,

"...Except ye repent, ye shall all likewise perish." (Luke 13:3). *"But as many as received him, to them gave he power to become the*

WHO IS JESUS?

sons of God, even to them that believe on his name:" (John 1:12).

God commands all men to repent, and therefore, all men can repent. No sin is excluded from God's forgiveness

"Who gave himself for us, that he might redeem us from all iniquity, and purify unto himself a peculiar people, zealous of good works." (Titus 2:14).

Therefore, man's need is clear,

"... Now is the accepted time; behold, now is the day of salvation." (2 Corinthians 6:2). *"Seek ye the Lord while he may be found, call ye upon him while he is near:"* (Isaiah 55:6). *"For whosoever shall call upon the name of the Lord shall be saved."* (Romans 10: 13). *"Who will have all men to be saved, and to come unto the knowledge of the truth. . . . Who gave himself a ransom for all, to be testified in due time."* (1 Timothy 2:4, 6).

God offers everyone salvation. If you have not trusted Christ as your Savior, why not admit you are a lost sinner, and ask Him to forgive you of your sins, and receive the Lord Jesus Christ as your Savior. Receive God's grace by accepting salvation by faith.

"For by grace are ye saved through faith; and that not of yourselves: it is the gift of God: not of works, lest any man should boast." (Ephesians 2:8-9).

SUMMING UP THE TEACHING

You may pray a simple prayer, honestly with all your heart:

"Dear Lord, I know that I am a sinner, but I am sorry for my sins. I believe that the Lord Jesus died for me and rose again, and with all my heart, I turn from my sin and receive Him as my Saviour right now. Thank you, Lord, for saving me! Amen."

Your prayer should come from your heart and truly believes and accepts God's offer of forgiveness of sin. It is not the prayer that saves, but the true intent of one's heart that truly believes.

> *"For with the heart man believeth unto righteousness; and with the mouth confession is made unto salvation."* (Romans 10:10)

God wants to save you. God never fails to keep His Word. Take God at His Word.

> *"But the word of the Lord endureth fore ever. And this is the word which by the gospel is preached unto you."* (1 Peter 1:25).

If I can be of help, please contact me by telephone or email. I will certainly try to help you to find Christ as your Savior.

WHO IS JESUS?

For a clear explanation of the Trinity, that God the Father, Son, and Holy Spirit are One God you can read my booklet "Understanding the Trinity" at:

> http://bibletruthbookstore.com/.
>
> Cooper P. Abrams, III
> Bible Truth Web Site
> http://bible-truth.org
> cpabrams3@gmail.com

My Web Site Bible-truth.org has more information concerning what the Bible teaches on many subjects. Go to http://bible-truth.org

www.ingramcontent.com/pod-product-compliance
Lightning Source LLC
Chambersburg PA
CBHW060425050426
42449CB00009B/2133